S0-BRY-904

# Secular Love

# Secular Love

Michael Ondaatje

*

COACH HOUSE PRESS
TORONTO

Copyright © Michael Ondaatje, 1984.
No part of this book may be used or reproduced in any way
without written permission except in the case of
brief quotations to be used in articles or reviews.

Front cover photograph by Dominic Sansoni.

Published with the assistance of the Canada Council
and the Ontario Arts Council.

OTHER BOOKS BY MICHAEL ONDAATJE

*The Dainty Monsters*
*The Man with 7 Toes*
*The Collected Works of Billy the Kid*
*Rat Jelly*
*Coming through Slaughter*
*Elimination Dance*
*There's a Trick with a Knife I'm Learning to Do: Poems '63-'78*
*Running in the Family*
*In the Skin of a Lion*

CANADIAN CATALOGUING IN PUBLICATION

Ondaatje, Michael, 1943-
Secular love.

Poems.

ISBN 0-88910-288-0

I. Title.

PS8529.N38S42 1942   C811'.54   C84-099521-9
PR9199.3054S42 1984

FIFTH PRINTING

This book is for Linda

\*

Tin Roof is for Phyllis Webb

Rock Bottom is for any hound dog's sake

'You're an actor, aren't you?'

The man nodded silently and averted his eyes.

'I've seen you in films. You always seem embarrassed at the thought of what you have to say next.'

The man laughed and again averted his eyes.

'Your trouble, I believe, is that you always hold back something of yourself. You're not shameless enough for an actor. In my opinion you should learn how to run properly and scream properly, with your mouth wide open. I've noticed that even when you yawn you're afraid to open your mouth all the way. In your next film make a sign to show that you've understood me. You haven't even been discovered yet. I'm looking forward to seeing you grow older from film to film.'

*Peter Handke*

# Contents

# Claude Glass

*claude glass*: a somewhat convex dark or coloured
hand-mirror, used to concentrate the features of
the landscape in subdued tones.

'Grey walked about everywhere with that
pretty toy, the claude glass, in his hand, making the
beautiful forms of the landscape compose in its
luscious chiaroscuro.' *Gosse* (1882)

\*

He is told about
the previous evening's behaviour.

Starting with a punchbowl
on the volleyball court.
Dancing and falling across coffee tables,
asking his son Are *you* the bastard
who keeps telling me I'm drunk?
kissing the limbs of women
suspicious of his friends serenading
five pigs by the barn
heaving a wine glass towards garden
and continually going through gates
into the dark fields
and collapsing.
His wife half carrying him home
rescuing him from departing cars,
complains this morning
of a sore shoulder.
                And even later
his thirteen year old daughter's struggle
to lift him into the back kitchen
after he has passed out, resting his head on rocks,
wondering what he was looking for in dark fields.

For he has always loved that ancient darkness
where the flat rocks glide like Japanese tables
where he can remove clothes
and lie with moonlight on the day's heat
hardened in stone, drowning
in this star blanket this sky
like a giant trout

conscious how the heaven
careens over him
as he moves in back fields
kissing the limbs of trees
or placing ear on stone which rocks him
and then stands to watch the house
in its oasis of light.
And he knows something is happening there to him
solitary while he spreads his arms
and holds everything that is slipping away together.

He is suddenly in the heat of the party
slouching towards women, revolving
round one unhappy shadow.
That friend who said he would find
the darkest place, and then wave.
He is not a lost drunk
like his father or his friend, can,
he says, stop on a dime, and he can
he could because even now, now in
this brilliant darkness where
grass has lost its colour and it's all
fucking Yeats and moonlight, he knows
this colourless grass is making his bare feet green
for it is the hour of magic
which no matter what sadness
leaves him grinning.

At certain hours of the night
ducks are nothing but landscape
just voices breaking as they nightmare.
The weasel wears their blood
home like a scarf,
cows drain over the horizon
                                    and the dark
vegetables hum onward underground

but the mouth
          wants  plum.

Moves from room to room
where brown beer glass
smashed lounges at his feet
opens the long rust stained gate
and steps towards invisible fields
that he knows from years of daylight.
He snorts in the breeze
which carries a smell
of cattle on its back.

What this place does not have
is the white paint of bathing cabins
the leak of eucalyptus.
During a full moon
outcrops of rock shine
skunks spray abstract into the air
cows burp as if practising
the name of Francis Ponge.
His drunk state wants the mesh of place.
Ludwig of Bavaria's Roof Garden –
glass plants, iron parrots
Venus Grottos, tarpaulins of Himalaya.
By the kitchen sink he tells someone
from now on I will drink only landscapes
– here, pour me a cup of Spain.

Opens the gate and stumbles
blood like a cassette through the body
away from the lights, unbuttoning,
this desire to be riverman.

Tentatively
            he recalls
his drunk invitation to the river.
He has steered the awesome car
past sugarbush to the blue night water
and steps out
speaking to branches
and the gulp of toads.
Subtle applause of animals.
A snake leaves a path
like temporary fossil.
                        He falls
back onto the intricacies
of gearshift and steering wheel
alive as his left arm
which now departs out of the window
trying to tug passing sumac
pine    bush    tamarack
into the car
            to the party.
Drunkenness opens his arms like a gate
and over the car invisible insects
ascend out of the beams like meteorite
crushed dust of the moon
... he waits for the magic star called Lorca.

On the front lawn a sheet
tacked across a horizontal branch.
A projector starts a parade
of journeys, landscapes, relatives,

friends leaping out within pebbles of water
caught by the machine as if creating rain.

Later when wind frees the sheet
and it collapses like powder in the grass
pictures fly without target
and howl their colours over Southern Ontario
clothing burdock
rhubarb a floating duck.
Landscapes and stories
flung into branches
and the dog walks under the hover of the swing
beam of the projection bursting in his left eye.
The falling sheet the star of Lorca swoops
someone gets up and heaves his glass
into the vegetable patch
towards the slow stupid career of beans.

This is the hour
when dead men sit
and write each other.
        "Concerning the words we never said
            during morning hours of the party
            there was glass under my bare feet
            laws of the kitchen were broken
            and each word moved
            in my mouth like muscle ..."

This is the hour for sudden journeying.
                Cervantes accepts
a 17th Century invitation
from the Chinese Emperor.
Schools of Chinese-Spanish Linguistics!
Rivers of the world meet!

And here
ducks dressed in Asia
pivot on foreign waters.


At 4 a.m. he wakes in the sheet
that earlier held tropics in its whiteness.

The invited river flows through the house
into the kitchen up
stairs, he awakens and moves within it.
In the dim light
he sees the turkish carpet under water,
low stools, glint
of piano pedals, even a sleeping dog
whose dreams may be of rain.

It is a river he has walked elsewhere
now visiting moving with him at the hip
to kitchen where a friend sleeps in a chair
head on the table his grip
still round a glass, legs underwater.

He wants to relax
and give in to the night
fall horizontal and swim
to the back kitchen where his daughter sleeps.
He wishes to swim
to each of his family and gaze
at their underwater dreaming
this magic chain of bubbles.
Wife, son, household guests, all
comfortable in clean river water.

He is aware that for hours
there has been no conversation,
tongues have slid to stupidity on alcohol
sleeping mouths are photographs of yells.

He stands waiting, the sentinel,
shambling back and forth, his anger
and desire against the dark
which, if he closes his eyes,
will lose them all.


                          The oven light
shines up through water at him
a bathysphere    a ghost ship
and in the half drowned room
the crickets like small pins
begin to tack down
the black canvas of this night,
begin to talk their hesitant
gnarled epigrams to each other
across the room.
                    Creak and echo.
Creak and echo. With absolute clarity
he knows where he is.

# Tin Roof

She hesitated. 'Are you being romantic now?'
'I'm trying to tell you how I feel without
exposing myself. You know what I mean?'
*Elmore Leonard*

\*

You stand still for three days
for a piece of wisdom
and everything falls to the right place

or wrong place

                    You speak
            don't know whether
seraph or bitch
flutters at your heart

and look through windows
for cue cards
blazing in the sky.
                    The solution.
This last year I was sure
I was going to die

*

The geography of this room    I know so well
tonight    I could rise in the dark
sit at the table    and write without light.
I am here in the country of warm rains.
A small cabin – a glass, wood,
tin bucket on the Pacific Rim.

                    Geckoes climb
the window to peer in,
and all day the tirade pale blue waves
touch the black shore of volcanic rock

and fall to pieces here

\*

How to arrive at this
drowning
on the edge of sea

      (How to drive
the Hana Road, he said –
one hand on the beer
one hand on your thigh
and one eye for the road)

Waves leap to this cliff all day
and in the evening lose
their pale blue

he rises from the bed
as wind from three directions
falls, takes his place
on the peninsula of sheets
which also loses colour

stands in the loose green kimono
by a large window and gazes

through gecko
past the deadfall
into sea,

      the unknown magic he loves
throws himself into

         the blue heart

*

Tell me
all you know
about bamboo

growing wild, green
growing up into soft arches
in the temple ground

the traditions

driven through hands
through the heart
during torture

and most of all

                    this

small bamboo pipe
not quite horizontal
that drips
every ten seconds
to a shallow bowl

I love this
being here
not a word
just the faint
fall of liquid
the boom of an iron buddhist bell
in the heart rapid
as ceremonial bamboo

\*

To be lost

A man buying wine
Rainier beer at the store
would he be satisfied with this?
Cold showers, electric skillet,
*Red River* on tv
Oh he could be

(Do you want
                    to be happy and write?)

He happens to love the stark
luxury of this place
– no armchairs, a fridge of beer and mangoes

            Precipitation.

To avoid a story        The refusal to move

All our narratives of sleep
a mild rumble to those inland

            Illicit pockets of
            the kimono

Heart like a sleeve

*

The cabin
            its tin roof
a wind run radio
catches the noise of the world.
He focuses on the gecko
almost transparent body
how he feels now
everything passing through him like light.
In certain mirrors
he cannot see himself at all.
He is joyous and breaking down.
The tug over the cliff.
What protects him
is the warmth in the sleeve

that is all, really

*

We go to the stark places of the earth
and find moral questions everywhere

Will John Wayne and Montgomery Clift
take their cattle to Missouri or Kansas?

Tonight I lean over the Pacific
and its blue wild silk
ringed by creatures
who
*tchick tchick tchick*
my sudden movement
who say nothing else.

There are those who are in
and there are those who look in

Tiny leather toes
hug the glass

*

On the porch
thin ceramic
chimes
　　　ride wind
off the Pacific

bells of the sea

　　　I do not know
the name of large orange flowers
which thrive on salt air
lean half drunk
against the steps

Untidy banana trees
thick moss on the cliff
and then the plunge
to black volcanic shore

It is impossible to enter the sea here
except in a violent way

　　　How we have moved
from thin ceramic

to such destruction

*

All night
          the touch

of wave on volcano.

There was the woman
who clutched my hair
like a shaken child.
The radio whistles
round a lost wave length.

All night slack-key music
and the bird whistling *duino*
duino, words and music
entangled in pebble
ocean static.
The wild sea and her civilization
the League of the Divine Wind
and traditions of death.

          Remember
those women in movies
who wept into the hair
of their dead men?

*

Going up stairs
I hang my shirt
on the stiff
ear of an antelope

Above the bed
          memory
restless green bamboo
          the distant army
assembles wooden spears

her feet braced
on the ceiling
sea in the eye

Reading the article
an 1825 report    *Physiologie du Gout*
on the artificial growing of truffles
speaks
          of "vain efforts
and deceitful promises,"
commandments of culinary art

Good
morning to your body
hello nipple
and appendix scar like a letter
of too much passion
from a mad Mexican doctor

All this noise at your neck!

heart clapping
like green bamboo

      this earring
    which
has flipped over
    and falls
        into the pool of your ear

The waves against black stone
that was a thousand year old
burning red river
could not reach us

\*

Cabin

'hana'

     this *flower* of wood
in which we rose
out of the blue sheets
you thin as horizon
reaching for lamp or book
my shirt

     hungry
for everything about the other

here we steal places to stay
as we steal time
     never too proud to beg,
even if we never
see the other's grin and star again

there is nothing resigned
in this briefness
we swallow complete

I will know everything here

     this cup
          balanced on my chest
     my eye witnessing the petal
     drop away from its order,
     your arm

for ever

precarious in all our fury

\*

Every place has its own wisdom. Come.
Time we talked about the sea,
the long waves
                    'trapped around islands'

*

There are maps now whose portraits
have nothing to do with surface

Remember the angels, floating compasses
– Portolan atlases so complex
we looked down and never knew
which was earth which was sea?
The way birds the colour of prairie
confused by the sky
flew into the earth
(Remember those women
who claimed dead miners
the colour of the coal they drowned in)

The bathymetric maps startle.
Visions of the ocean floor
troughs, naked blue deserts,
Ganges Cone, the Mascarene Basin

so one is able now
in ideal situations
to plot a stroll
to new continents
'doing the Berryman walk'

And beneath the sea
there are
these giant scratches
of pain
the markings of
some perfect animal
who has descended
burying itself
under the glossy
ballroom

or they have to do with ascending,
what we were, the earth creatures
longing for horizon.
I know one thing
our sure non-sliding
civilized feet
our small leather shoes
did not make them

(Ah you should be happy and write)

I want the passion
which puts your feet on the ceiling
this fist
to smash forward

take this silk
          somehow   *Ah*
out of the rooms of poetry


(Listen, solitude, X wrote,
 is not an absolute,
 it is just a resting place)

listen    in the end
the pivot from angel to witch
depends on small things
this animal, the question
are you happy?

No I am not happy

lucky though

✳

Rainy Night Talk

Here's to
the overlooked
nipples of Spain
          brown Madrid aureoles
kneecaps of Ohio girls
kneeling in the palms of men
waiting to be thrown high
into the clouds
of a football stadium

          Here's to
the long legged
woman from Kansas
whispering good morning at 5,
          dazed
in balcony moonlight

All that drizzle the night before
walking walking through rain
slam her car door
and wrote my hunger out, the balcony
like an entrance
to a city of suicides.

Here's to the long legs
driving home
in more and more rain
weaving like a one-sided
lonely conversation
over the mountains

And what were you
carrying? in your head
that night Miss
Souri? Miss Kansas?

while I put my hands
sweating
on the cold
window
on the edge
of the trough of this city?

\*

Breaking down after logical rules
couldn't be the hit and run driver
I wanted Frank Sinatra
I was thinking blue pyjamas
I was brought up on movies and song!

I could write my suite of poems
for Bogart    drunk
six months after the departure at Casablanca.
I see him lying under the fan
at the Slavyansky Bazar Hotel
and soon he will see the truth
the stupidity of his gesture
he'll see it in the space
between the whirling metal.

                Stupid fucker
he says to himself, stupid fucker
and knocks the bottle
leaning against his bare stomach
onto the sheet. Gin stems
out like a four leaf clover.
I used to be lucky he says
I had white suits black friends
who played the piano ...
                                and that
was a movie I saw just once.

What about Burt Lancaster
limping away at the end of *Trapeze?*
Born in 1943. And I saw that six times.

(I grew up knowing I could never fly)


That's me. You. Educated
at the *Bijou*. And don't ask me
about my interpretation of "Madame George."
That's a nine minute song
a two hour story.

So how do we discuss
the education of our children?
Teach them to be romantics
to veer towards the sentimental?
Toss them into the air like Tony Curtis
and make 'em do the triple somersault
through all these complexities
and commandments?

*

Oh Rilke, I want to sit down calm like you
or pace the castle, avoiding the path of the cook, Carlo,
who believes down to his turnip soup
that you speak the voice of the devil.
I want the long lines my friend spoke of
that bamboo which sways muttering
like wooden teeth in the slim volume I have
with its childlike drawing of Duino Castle.
I have circled your book for years
like a wave combing
the green hair of the sea
kept it with me, your name
a password in the alley.
I always wanted poetry to be that
but this solitude brings no wisdom
just two day old food in the fridge,
certain habits you would not approve of.
If I said all of your name now
it would be the movement
of the tide you soared over
so your private angel
could become part of a map.

I am too often busy with things
I wish to get away from, and I want
the line to move slowly now, slow
-ly like a careful drunk across the street
no cars in the vicinity
but in his fearful imagination.
How can I link your flowing name
to geckoes or a slice of octopus?
Though there are Rainier beer cans,
magically, on the windowsill.

And still your lovely letters
January 1912 near Trieste.
The car you were driven in
'at a snail's pace'
through Provence. Wanting
'to go into chrysalis ...
to live by the heart and nothing else.'
Or your guilt –

           'I howl at the moon
           with all my heart
           and put the blame
           on the dogs'

I can see you sitting down
the suspicious cook asleep
so it is just you
and the machinery of the night
that foul beast that sucks and drains
leaping over us sweeping our determination
away with its tail. Us and the coffee,
all the small charms we invade it with.

As at midnight we remember the colour
of the dogwood flower growing
like a woman's sex outside the window.
I wanted poetry to be walnuts
in their green cases
but now it is the sea
and we let it drown us,
and we fly to it released
by giant catapults
of pain loneliness deceit and vanity

# Rock Bottom

I

O lady hear me. I have no

other
voice left.

*Robert Creeley*

\*

2 a.m.   The moonlight
in the kitchen

Will this be
*testamentum porcelli*?
Unblemished art and truth
whole hog   the pig's testament
what I know of passion
having written of it
seen my dog shiver
with love and disappear
crazy into trees

                    I want

the woman whose face
I could not believe in the moonlight
her mouth forever as horizon

                    and both of us
grim with situation


now
suddenly
we reside
near the delicate
heart
of Billie Holiday

*

You said, this
doesn't happen so quick
I must remind you of someone

        No,
though I am seduced
by this light, and
frantic arguments
on the porch,
I ain't subtle
you run rings
round me

           but this quietness
white dress    long legs
arguing your body
away from me

and I with all the hunger
I didn't know I had

* *(Inner Tube)*


On the warm July river
head back

upside down river
for a roof

slowly paddling
towards an estuary between trees

there's a dog
learning to swim near me
friends on shore

my head
dips
back to the eyebrow
I'm the prow
on an ancient vessel,
this afternoon
I'm going down to Peru
soul between my teeth

a blue heron
with its awkward
broken backed flap
upside down

one of us is wrong

he
in his blue grey thud
thinking he knows
the blue way
out of here

or me

* *('The space in which we have dissolved – does it taste of us?')*

Summer night came out of the water
climbed into my car and drove home
got out of the car still wet towel round me
opened the gate and walked to the house

Disintegration of the spirit
no stars
leaf being eaten by moonlight

The small creatures who are blind
who travel with the aid
of petite white horns
take over the world

Sound of a moth

The screen door in its suspicion
allows nothing in, as I allow nothing in.
The raspberries my son gave me
wild, cold out of the fridge, a few I put
in my mouth, some in my shirt pocket
and forgot

I sit here
in a half dark kitchen
the stain at my heart
caused by this gift

*(Daily News)*

Brown grass
hoppers jumping
all day    all night
dolphins of the drought

something is going wrong here
they bombed us with dragon flies
who mated with grasshoppers
and now things leap
out of the earth
and try to fly

certain stories I told you were true
the woman with the 200 pound tumor
the person whose career is
jacking off turkeys
in Kitchener Waterloo
the pig who swallowed
my daughter's gold ring
and went mad
from vanity

*  *(Saturday)*

The three trunks
of the walnut

the ceremonial ducks
who limbo under the fence
and creep up the lawn

Apple tree    Blue and white house
I know this is beautiful

I wished to write today
about small things
that might persuade me
out of my want

The lines I read
about 'cowardice' and 'loyalty'
I don't know
if this is drowning
or coming up for air

          At night
I give you my hand
like a corpse
out of the water

\*

A line in my friend's song

*I've got friends
till the cows come home*

Sometimes these songs
loosen my heart
more than reality,
hold back the spider
crawling off
the centre of the web

this arc of the heart
to the Pacific

*In five more years
I will rise on the wings of song*

\* *(Insomnia)*

Night and its forces
step through the picket gate
from the blue bush
to the kitchen

Everywhere it moves
and we cannot sleep we cannot sleep
we damn the missionaries
their morals thin as stars
we find ourselves
within the black
circus of the fly
all night long
his sandpaper
tabasco leg

The dog sleepwalks
into the cupboard
into the garden and heart attacks
hello
I've had a dog dream
wake up and cannot find
my long ears

Nicotine    caffeine
hungry bodies
could put us to sleep
but nothing puts us to sleep
except devastation

\*

How many windows have I broken?
And doors and lamps, and last month
a tumbler I smashed into a desk

then stood over the sink
digging out splinters
with an awkward left hand
I have beaten my head with stones
pieces of fence
tried to tear out my eyes
these are not exaggerations
they were acts when words failed
the way surgeons
hammer hearts gone still

now this
small parallel pain
in my finger
the invisible thing inside
circling
             glass
             on its voyage out
             to the heart

*If you love me and think only of me*
*lift your robe and ford the river Chen*

catch
  'the floating world'
8:52 from Chicago

lift your skirt
through customs,

kiss me in the parking lot

*  (*'La Belle Romance'*)


Another deep night
with the National Enquirer

silence

like the unseen
arms of a bat

the book
falls open
to sadness
– dead flowers, dead
horses who carried
lovers to a meeting

On my last walk
through the kitchen
I see it

                I lift
huge arms of a cobweb
out of the air
and carry its Y
slowly to the porch
as if alive

as if it was a wounded bird
or some terrible camouflaged insect
that could damage children

\*

We. Were. Talking. About. The. Aenead.
I. Said. It. Was. A. Terrible. Book.
That. I. Hated. Aeneas.
F. Said. Yeah. He. Keeps. All. His.
Troubles. To. Himself.
S. Glanced. At. Me. And. Said.
I. Don't. Know. Why. You. Should.
Dislike. Him. Then.

\*

The distance between us
and then this small map
of stars
          a concentrated
ocean of the night

when lovers worship heavens
they are worshipping
a lack of distance

my brother the moon
the lofty mattress
of nebula,
rash and spray of love

          It is all
as close as my palm
on your body

                    so you
among pillows and moonlight
look up, search
for the jewellery
bathing in darkness

satellite hunger, remote control,
'the royal we'

          and find
your own dark hand

\* *(Envoi)*


Tonight a meticulous galaxy

       Hunger
evaporates
         climbs
this tree of stars
map of the dreadful night

stretches itself
over Atlantic and Pacific
over the noisy tropic leaf
over two children
and a woman driving

so this gratitude
friendship and
a little lust
for her left thigh via you

**2**

While this moon is occupied each player may make no comment or gesture about a player's past game performance or future game potential except to disparage his own or to admire that of another.

from *Cosmic Encounter,*
*rules to Expansion Set #5*

*

What were the names of the towns
we drove into and through

        stunned    lost

having drunk our way
up vineyards
and then Hot Springs
boiling out the drunkenness

What were the names
I slept through
        my head
on your thigh
hundreds of miles

of blackness entering the car

        All this
        darkness and stars
but now
under the Napa Valley night
a star arch of dashboard
the ripe grape moon
we are together
and I love this muscle

I love this muscle
that tenses
        and joins
the accelerator
to my cheek

– and sometimes
I think
women in novels are too
controlled by the adverb.
As they depart
a perfume of description

'She rose from the table
and left her shoe
behind, *casually*'

'Let's keep our minds
clear, she said drunkenly,'
the print hardly dry
on words like that

My problem tonight
is this landscape.
Like the sanskrit lover
who sees breasts in the high clouds,
testicles on the riverbed
('The soldiers left their balls
behind, crossing into Bangalore
she said, mournfully')

Every leaf bends
I can put my hand
into various hollows, the dogs
lick their way up the ditch
swallow the scent
of whatever they eat

*Always* wanted to own
a movie theatre
called 'The Moonlight'

What's playing at *The Moonlight*
she asked
leafily

Men never trail away.
They sweat adjective.
'She fell into
his unexpected arms.'
He mixes a 'devious' drink.
He spills his maddened seed
onto the lettuce —

*  (Real Life)


In real life
men talk about art
women judge men

In the Queen Street tavern
3 p.m. the only one busy
is the waitress
who reads a book a day

Hour of the afternoon soaps

Accusations
which hide the trap
door of tomorrow's guilt.
Men bursting into bedrooms
out of restaurants.
Everyone talks on phones
to the lover's brother
or the husband's mistress

My second beer
my fifth cigarette
the only thing more
confusing venomous
than real life
is this frantic hour
where nobody smokes
and nobody talks about art

I've woken in thick
households
all my life
but can nightmare myself
into this future –
last spring I sat here
Sunday Morning
as bachelor drunks
came in, eyes
in prayer to the Billy Graham Show

The pastel bar
grey colours of the tv
this is where people come
after the second failure of redemption

Ramon Fernandez,
                    tell me
what port you
bought that tattoo

*

Midnight dinner at the *Vesta Lunch*

Here there is nothing
I have taken from you
so I begin with memory
as old songs do
                    in this café
against the night

in this villa refrain
where we collect the fragment
no longer near us
to make ourselves whole

                    your bright eyes
in a greek bar, the way
you wear your hat

*

I have always
been afflicted
by angular
small breasted
women
from the mid west,

knew this was true
the minute I met you

*

A fragment of glass in my finger
This arm over your shoulder

Someday maybe I'll charm you
with a suit, matching socks
now everything's in hock
for this moment somewhere
where disciplines
bewilder us, let us go
under
         loons going blind
going nowhere
murmuring heartbeat heartbeat

＊

Repetition of midnight
Every creature doth sleep
But us

and the fanatics

A green kimono
                some photographs
this maple spile

            I want
the roulette of the lightning bolt
to decide all

On this suburban street
the skate-boarder rolls
surrounded by the seeming
hiss of electricity
                unlit
I see him through the trees
up Ptarmigan
                a thick sweater
for the late September night

I am unable to make anything of this
who are these words for

Even the dog
curls away
into himself
the only one to know your name

*

I write about you
as if I own you
which I do not.
As you can say of nothing
this is mine.

When we rise
the last hug
no longer belongs,
is your fiction
or my story.
Mulch for the future.

Whether we pass
through each other
like pure arrows
or fade into rumour
I write down now
a fiction of your arm

or of that afternoon
in Union Station
when we both were lost
pain falling free
the speed of tears
under the Grand Rotunda
as we disappeared
rose from each other

you and your arrow
taking just
what you fled through

\* (*'I want to be lifted up by some great*
*white bird unknown to the police ...'*)


I will never let a chicken
into my life
but I have let you
though you squeezed in
through a screen door
the way some chickens do

I would never let chickens
influence my character
but like them good sense
scatters at your entrance
– 'poetic skill,' 'duty,'
under the fence

Your lean shoulders
studied with greyhounds.
Such ball and socket joints
I've seen only in diagrams
on the cover of *Scientific American*.
I've let greyhounds
into my vicinity
– noses, paws, ribcages
against my arm, I admit
a weakness
for reluctant modesty.
I could spend days lying on the ground
seeing the world with the perspective of snails
stumbling the small territory of obsessions
this leaf and grain of you,
could attempt the epic
journey over your shoulder.

When you were a hotel gypsy
delirious by windows
waving your arms
and singing over the parking lots
I learned from the foolish oyster
and stepped out.
So here I am
saying see this
look what I found
when I opened myself up
before death before the world,
look at this blue eye
this socket in her waving arm
these wonders.

In the night busy as snails
in wet chlorophyll apartments
we enter each other's shells
the way humans at such times
wish to enter mouths of lovers,

sleeping like the rumour of pearl
in the embrace of oyster.

I have never let spectacles into my life
and now I am walking past
where I could see.
Here,
          where the horizon was

\* *(The Desire Under the Elms Motel)*

how I attempted seduction
with a select and
careful playing of
The McGarrigle Sisters

how you seduced me
stereophonically      the laugh

the nose      ankle      nature

    repartee    the knee

your sad determination      letters

the earring

        that falls

        *'hey love –*

         *you forgot your glove'*

\*

and now
if it was Chopin
at the wheel
would we hunger less?

The bad moon rising anyway

My tin ear
would still play
into your hand

some charms

\*

Speaking to you
this hour
these days when
I have lost the feather of poetry
and the rains
of separation
surround us tock
tock like *Go* tablets

Everyone has learned
to move carefully

'Dancing'   'laughing'   'bad taste'
is a memory
a tableau behind trees of law

In the midst of love for you
my wife's suffering
anger in every direction
and the children wise
as tough shrubs
but they are not tough
– so I fear
how anything can grow from this

all the wise blood
poured from little cuts
down into the sink

this hour it is not
your body I want
but your quiet company

\*

Dentists disguise their own bad teeth
barbers go bald, foolish birds
travel to one particular tree.
They pride themselves
on focus.
Poets cannot spell.
Everyone claims abstinence.

Reading Neruda to a class
reading his lovely old
curiosity about all things
I am told this is the first time
in months I seem happy.
Jealous of his slide
through complexity.
All afternoon I keep
stepping into his pocket

       whispering
instruct and delight me

*  *(These back alleys)*
                                  *for Daphne*


In '64 you moved
and where was I?
– somewhere and married.
(In '64 everybody got married)

Whatever we are now we were then.
Some days those maps collide
falling into future land.
It seems for hours
we have sat in your car,
almost valentine's day,
I've got a plane to meet and I
hold your rose for you.
This talking
like a slow dance,
the sharing of earphones.

Since I got separated
I cannot hold
my brain in my arms anymore.
Sitting in the back alley
this new mapping, hello
to the terra nova.
Now we watch each other
in our slow walks towards
and out of everything
we wanted to know in '64

\*

and for George moonlight
became her. curious, after years of wit
he saw it enter her and believed,
singing love songs in the back seat.

Three of us drive downtown
in our confusions

goodbye to the hills of the 30's

sinned. torn apart, how do each of us
share our hearts

and George still 'hearty,' bad jokes
scattering to the group,
does not converse, but he sings the heartbreakers
badly and precisely in the back seat

*so we moon, we tough*

*

Kissing the stomach
kissing your scarred
skin boat. History
is what you've travelled on
and take with you

We've each had our stomachs
kissed by strangers
to the other

and as for me
I bless everyone
who kissed you here

*  (*Ends of the Earth*)


      For you I have slept
like a pure arrow in the hall
pointing towards your wakefulness
... a few misdemeanors but otherwise
lost without your company, you
in intricate time zones

      And wary
piece by piece
we put each other together
              your past
that of one who has walked
through fifteen strange houses
in order to be here

the charm of Wichita
gunmen in your bones
        the 19th century
strolling like a storm
through your long body

that history I read in comic books
and on the flickering screen
when I was thirteen

Now we are cats-cradled
in the Pacific
how does one avoid this?
Go to the ends of the earth?
The loose moon follows

            Wet moonlight
            recalls childhood

the long legged daughter
the stars    the lights
of Wichita in the distance

midnight and hugging
against her small chest
the favourite book,
*Goodnight Moon*

under the covers she
reads its courtly order
its list of farewells
to everything

                        We grow less complex
We reduce ourselves      The way lovers
have their small cheap charms
silver lizard,
a stone

Ancient customs
that grow from dust
                   swirled out
from prairie into tropic

Strange how the odours meet

How, however briefly, bedraggled
history
        focusses

# Skin Boat

On one occasion on the Alaska Peninsula, I heard thin squeaky voices in the tall grass. I watched quietly and had glimpses of tiny forms flashing by the little openings in the dense cover. I could only guess what might be the intimate affairs of those diminutive mammals.

Olaus J. Murie, *A Field Guide to Animal Tracks*

## Her House

Because she has lived alone, her house is the product of nothing but herself and necessity. The necessity of growing older and raising children. Others drifted into her life, in and out and they have changed her, added things, but I have never been into a home that is a revelation of character and time as much as hers. It contains those she knows and has known and she has distilled all of her journey. When I first met her I saw nothing but her, and now, as she becomes familiar, I recognise the small customs.

The problem for her is leaving. She says, 'Last night I was listening to everything I know so well, and I imagined what if I woke up in a year's time and there were different trees.' Streets, the weight of sea air, certain birds who recognise your shrubbery, that too holds you, allows a freedom of habit, is a house.

*

Everything here is alien to me but you. And your room like a grey well, your coat hangers above the laundry machine where you hang the semi-damp clothes so you do not have to iron them, the green grey walls of wood, the secret drawer which you opened after you knew me two years to show me the ancient Japanese pens. All this I love. Though I carry my own landscape in me and my three bags. But this has become your skin, and as you leave you recognise this.

On certain evenings, when I have not bothered to put on lights, I hit my knees on low bookcases where they should not be. But you shift your hip easily, habitually, around them as you pass by carrying laundry or books. When you can move through a house blindfolded it belongs to you. You are moving like blood calmly within your own body. It is only recently that I am able to wake beside you and without looking, almost in a dream, put out my hand and know exactly where your shoulder or your heart will be – you in your specific posture in this bed of yours that we share. And at times this has seemed to be knowledge. As if you were a blueprint of your house.

## The Cinnamon Peeler

If I were a cinnamon peeler
I would ride your bed
and leave the yellow bark dust
on your pillow.

Your breasts and shoulders would reek
you could never walk through markets
without the profession of my fingers
floating over you. The blind would
stumble certain of whom they approached
though you might bathe
under rain gutters, monsoon.

Here on the upper thigh
at this smooth pasture
neighbour to your hair
or the crease
that cuts your back. This ankle.
You will be known among strangers
as the cinnamon peeler's wife.

I could hardly glance at you
before marriage
never touch you
– your keen nosed mother, your rough brothers.
I buried my hands
in saffron, disguised them
over smoking tar,
helped the honey gatherers ...

*

When we swam once
I touched you in water
and our bodies remained free,
you could hold me and be blind of smell.
You climbed the bank and said

        this is how you touch other women
the grass cutter's wife, the lime burner's daughter.
And you searched your arms
for the missing perfume
           and knew

        what good is it
to be the lime burner's daughter
left with no trace
as if not spoken to in the act of love
as if wounded without the pleasure of a scar.

You touched
your belly to my hands
in the dry air and said
I am the cinnamon
peeler's wife. Smell me.

# Women like You

*the communal poem – Sigiri Graffiti, 5th century*

They do not stir
these ladies of the mountain
do not give us
the twitch of eyelids

                       The king is dead

They answer no one
take the hard
rock as lover.
Women like you
make men pour out their hearts

                       'Seeing you I want
                         no other life'

                       'The golden skins have
                        caught my mind'

who came here
out of the bleached land
climbed this fortress
to adore the rock
and with the solitude of the air
behind them
                carved an alphabet
whose motive was perfect desire

wanting these portraits of women
to speak
and caress

Hundreds of small verses
by different hands
became one
habit of the unrequited

Seeing you
I want no other life
and turn around
to the sky
and everywhere below
jungle, waves of heat
secular love

Holding the new flowers
a circle of
first finger and thumb
which is a window

to your breast

pleasure of the skin
earring   earring
curl
of the belly
                and then
stone mermaid
stone heart
dry as a flower
on rock
you long eyed women

the golden
drunk swan breasts
lips
the long long eyes

we stand against the sky

I bring you

a flute
from the throat
of a loon

so talk to me
of the used heart

## The River Neighbour

All these rumours. You lodge in the mountains
of Hang-chou, a cabin in Portland township,
or in Yüeh-chou for sure

the dust from my marriage
wasted our clear autumn

This month the cactus
under the rains

while you lounge with my children
by the creek snakes, the field asparagus

Across the universe
each room I lit
was a dark garden, I held
nothing but the lamp

this letter paints me
transparent as I am

One dead bird in the hall
conversation of the water-closets
company of the leaf on the stairs

I pass her often

Moon    leaf    memory of asparagus
I find her earrings
at the foot of curtainless windows

In the kitchen
salt fills the body
of an RCA Victor dog

Let us nose our way
next year with the spring waters
and search for each other
somewhere in the east

## To a Sad Daughter

All night long the hockey pictures
gaze down at you
sleeping in your tracksuit.
Belligerent goalies are your ideal.
Threats of being traded
cuts and wounds
– all this pleases you.
*O my god!* you say at breakfast
reading the sports page over the Alpen
as another player breaks his ankle
or assaults the coach.

When I thought of daughters
I wasn't expecting this
but I like this more.
I like all your faults
even your purple moods
when you retreat from everyone
to sit in bed under a quilt.
And when I say 'like'
I mean of course 'love'
but that embarrasses you.
You who feel superior to black and white movies
(coaxed for hours to see *Casablanca*)
though you were moved
by *Creature from the Black Lagoon*.

One day I'll come swimming
beside your ship or someone will
and if you hear the siren
listen to it. For if you close your ears
only nothing happens. You will never change.

I don't care if you risk
your life to angry goalies
creatures with webbed feet.
You can enter their caves and castles
their glass laboratories. Just
don't be fooled by anyone but yourself.

This is the first lecture I've given you.
You're 'sweet sixteen' you said.
I'd rather be your closest friend
than your father. I'm not good at advice
you know that, but ride
the ceremonies
until they grow dark.

Sometimes you are so busy
discovering your friends
I ache with a loss
– but that is greed.
And sometimes I've gone
into *my* purple world
and lost you.

One afternoon I stepped
into your room. You were sitting
at the desk where I now write this.
Forsythia outside the window
and sun spilled over you
like a thick yellow miracle
as if another planet
was coaxing you out of the house
– all those possible worlds! –
and you, meanwhile, busy with mathematics.

I cannot look at forsythia now
without loss, or joy for you.
You step delicately
into the wild world
and your real prize will be
the frantic search.
Want everything. If you break
break going out not in.
How you live your life I don't care
but I'll sell my arms for you,
hold your secrets forever.

If I speak of death
which you fear now, greatly,
it is without answers,
except that each
one we know is
in our blood.
Don't recall graves.
Memory is permanent.
Remember the afternoon's
yellow suburban annunciation.
Your goalie
in his frightening mask
dreams perhaps
of gentleness.

## All along the Mazinaw

Later the osprey

falling towards
only what he sees

the messenger heron
warning of our progress
up Mud Lake

a paddle is
stranger
to what it heaves out of the way

Wherever you go
within a silence
is witnessed,
                    touches.
Everything aware
of alteration but you.
Creatures who veer. The torn leaf
descending into marsh gas
into an ancient breath.

In bony rapids
rock gazed up
with the bright paint
of previous canoes.

But now, you, *c'est là,*
with the clear river water heart
the rock who floats
on her own deep reflection.

Female rock. Limb. Holes of hunger
we climb into and disappear.

One hour in the arms of the Mazinaw.

Those things we don't know we love
we love harder.
                    Tanned face
stern rock    the rock lolling
memorized by the Algonquin
Mohawk lovers. Mineral eye.

O yes I saw your dear sisters too
before this afternoon's passion
those depot creek nights when they
unpacked their breasts
serious and full of the fever of loon
for whoever stumbled
young onto the august
country waters.

## Pacific Letter

*to Stan of Depot Creek, old friend, pal o' mine*


Now I remember that you rebuilt my chicken coop
north of the farmhouse along the pasture fence
with fresh pine from Verona.
In autumn you hid a secret message under floorboards
knowing we would find it in spring.
A fanciful message. Carved with care.
As you carved you imagined the laughing.
We both know the pleasures art and making bring.

And in summer we lounged for month on month
letting slide the publishers and English Departments
who sent concerned letters that slept in the red mailbox.
Men and women came drifting in
from the sea and from the west border
and with them there was nothing at cross purpose.
They made nothing of mountain crossing
to share that fellowship.
The girls danced because
their long sleeves would not keep still
and I, drunk, went to sleep among field rocks.
We spoke out desires without regret.
Then you returned to the west of the province
and I to the south.

After separation had come to its worst
we met and travelled the Mazinaw with my sons
through all the thirty-six folds of that creature river
into the valley of bright lichen,
green rice beds, marble rock, and at night
slept under croaking pine.
The spirit so high it was all over the heavens!

And at Depot Creek we walked
for a last time down river
to a neighbour's southern boundary
past the tent where you composed verses
past the land where I once lived
the water about it clear in my memory as blue jade.
Then you and your wife sang back and forth
in the mosquito filled cabin under the naphtha.
The muskrat, listening at the edge,
heard our sound – guitars and lone violin
whose weavings seduced us with a sadness.

The canoe brushed over open lake
hearing the lighted homes
whose laughter eliminated the paddle
and the loon stumbled
up sudden into the air beside the boat
shocked us awake and disappeared
leaving a ripple that slid the moon away.
And before the last days in August
we scattered like stars and rain.

And I think now that this
is what we are to each other,
friends busy with their own distance
who reappear now and then alongside.
As once you could not believe
I had visited the town of your youth
where you sat in your room
perfecting *Heartbreak Hotel*
that new place to 'dwell' – that
gentle word in the midst of angry song.

All this comes to an end.
During summer evenings
I miss your company.
Things we clung to
stay on the horizon
and we become the loon
on his journey
a lone tropical taxi
to confused depth and privacy.

At such times – no talking
no conclusion in the heart.

I buy postage
                    seal this

and send it a thousand miles, thinking.

*Translations of my Postcards*

the peacock means order
the fighting kangaroos mean madness
the oasis means I have struck water

positioning of the stamp – the despot's head
horizontal, or 'mounted policemen,'
mean political danger

the false date means I
am not where I should be

when I speak of the weather
I mean business

a blank postcard says
I am in the wilderness

## A Dog in San Francisco

Sitting in an empty house
with a dog from the Mexican Circus!
O Daisy, embrace is my only pleasure.
Holding and hugging my friends. Education.
A wave of eucalyptus. Warm granite.
These are the things I have in my heart.
Heart and skills, there's nothing else.

I usually don't like small dogs but you
like midwestern women take over the air.
You leap into the air and pivot
a diver going up! You are known
to open the fridge and eat when you wish
you can roll down car windows and step out
you know when to get off the elevator.

I always wanted to be a dog
but I hesitated
for I thought they lacked certain skills.
Now I want to be a dog.

# 7 or 8 Things I Know About Her / A Stolen Biography

### The Father's Guns

After her father died they found nine guns in the house. Two in his clothing drawers, one under the bed, one in the glove compartment of the car, etc. Her brother took their mother out onto the prairie with a revolver and taught her to shoot.

### The Bird

For a while in Topeka parrots were very popular. Her father was given one in lieu of a payment and kept it with him at all times because it was the fashion. It swung above him in the law office and drove back with him in the car at night. At parties friends would bring their parrots and make them perform what they had been taught: the first line from *Twelfth Night,* a bit of Italian opera, cowboy songs, or a surprisingly good rendition of Russ Colombo singing "Prisoner of Love." Her father's parrot could only imitate the office typewriter, along with the *ching* at the end of each line. Later it broke its neck crashing into a bookcase.

### The Bread

Four miles out of Topeka on the highway – the largest electrical billboard in the State of Kansas. The envy of all Missouri. It advertised bread and the electrical image of a knife cut slice after slice. These curled off endlessly. 'Meet you at the bread,' 'See you at the loaf,' were common phrases. Aroused couples would park there under the stars on the open night prairie. Virtue was lost, "kissed all over by every boy in Wichita." Poets, the inevitable visiting writers, were taken to see it, and it hummed over the seductions in cars, over the nightmares of girls in bed. Slice after slice fell towards the earth. A feeding of the multitude in this parched land on the way to Dorrance, Kansas.

### First Criticism

She is two weeks old, her mother takes her for a drive. At the gas station the mechanic is cleaning the windshield and watches them through the glass. Wiping his hands he puts his head in the side window and says, 'Excuse me for saying this but I know what I'm talking about – that child has a heart condition.'

### Listening In

Overhear her in the bathroom, talking to a bug: 'I don't want you on me, honey.' 8 a.m.

### Self-Criticism

'For a while there was something about me that had a dubious quality. Dogs would not take meat out of my hand. The town bully kept handcuffing me to trees.'

### Fantasies

Always one fantasy. To be travelling down the street and a man in a clean white suit (the detail of 'clean' impresses me) leaps into her path holding flowers and sings to her while an invisible orchestra accompanies his solo. All her life she has waited for this and it never happens.

*Reprise*

In 1956 the electric billboard in Kansas caught fire and smoke plumed into a wild sunset. Bread on fire, broken glass. Birds flew towards it above the cars that circled round to watch. And last night, past midnight, her excited phone call. Her home town is having a marathon to benefit the symphony. She pays $4 to participate. A tuxedoed gentleman begins the race with a clash of cymbals and she takes off. Along the route at frequent intervals are quartets who play for her. When they stop for water a violinist performs a solo. So here she comes. And there I go, stepping forward in my white suit, with a song in my heart.

# Bessie Smith at Roy Thomson Hall

At first she refused to sing.

She had applied for the one concert – that she was allowed each sabbatical – to take place in Havana. Palms! Oh Pink Walls! Cuba! she would hum to herself, dazzling within the clouds.

But here she was. Given the choice of nine Honest Ed restaurants and then hurried to Roy Thomson Hall which certainly should never have been called that.

> A long brown dress, with fringes.
> Fred Longshaw at the piano.

She opened the first set with "Kitchen Man." Five people left. Al Neil had flown in from Vancouver on a tip. For the next ten minutes, after people realised it really *was* Bessie Smith, the hall was filled with shouted requests. "Any Woman's Blues," "Down in the Dumps" ... until she said I want to sing what I never was allowed to, because I died. And she brought the rest of the twentieth century under her wing.

She wore wings. They raised themselves with her arms each time she coaxed a phrase. Her wings would float up and fall slow like a hand held out of a car coming down against the wind, the feathers black as the Steinway. You should have been there.

During the intermission the stunned audience just sat in their seats. 'She's looking good' was one of the common remarks.

When she returned she brought out the band. They were glad to have arrived on earth, but they too had hoped for Havana. Abraham Wheat on soprano sax was there. Joe Smith on cornet was there. By midnight her voice was even better. She talked more between songs.

At 2 a.m. the band levitated. She used no microphone. Above us banners waved and danced like a multitude. She took on and caressed the songs of Jerome Kern. She asked what happened to her friend Charlie Green. And then, to her surprise, to apologise for Toronto, Charlie Green was allowed to join her. He had been found frozen in a Harlem tenement but now stepped forward shyly with his trombone. And now he and Joe Smith and Bessie Smith were alone on stage the audience quiet and the banners still and the air conditioning holding its breath. They wheeled away the Steinway. They brought out an old upright decorated with bullet holes. Al Neil was asked to sit in. She sang, "It won't be You."

The encore was made up of two songs. "Weeping Willow Blues" and "Far Away Blues." We stood like sudden wheat. But she could not hear us. She could not see us. Then she died again.

## The Concessions

*i.*

Wawanosh.
         In the corn of night
surrounded by the dusty dark green
hot insects and moon
             a star coat.

We are new and ancient here
talking through midnight's
tired arms,
letting go the newness.
I am home.
Old farmhouse, a defunct red truck
under the trees
conversation all evening
and I have nothing more to say
but this is a magic night.
Our bodies betray us, long for sleep.
Still – talk about the bear, the cause
of theatre, the first time we all met.

A yellow light falls onto the sink
and our arms lean forward
towards Elmira coffee cake.
Hello again, after Pacific months,
and I brought you a seed I never gave you
and I brought you stories and a peace I want
to give, but it is both of you
who bring comfort and friendship.

All night we are at this table.
              Tableau of faint light,
fragment of Ontario.
We would be plotting revolution in the 1830's.
And outside the same heat, old coat of stars,
the released lung of the country, and
great Ontario night beans growing
towards Goderich.
                    Lone houses
betrayed by poplar
reached only by long arms
of Wawanosh concessions,
the crow of night.


                 Tomorrow
will be all highway
till I get home.
Go to bed, exhausted and alone.
Go to bed with each others' minds.
I do not know what to say
about this kind of love
but I refuse to lose it.

*ii.*

By the outhouse and red truck
I look up towards a lit window
which seeps a yellow road into trees.
To end in the warm
glove of a maple!
*A bear.*
Welcome Shakespeare, Sarah Bernhardt,
someone is starting a new story.
Someone is dancing new on this
terrific ancient earth, claiming this
for mute ancestors
and their language of hands.
              The entertainers
who allow themselves long evenings
while others sleep.
The suspicious work of the community.

The town of Molesworth
which once housed a dancing cow
articulated us. As did the director
from Atwood, the fiddler from Listowel,
and the actress from Fergus, the writer from Wingham,
the mystic from Millbank.
These country hearts, a county conspiracy.
Their determined self-portraits
where alone one picks
up the pencil, begins with nothing
but these blank pages.
Let me tell you, I love them more and more
– all their night silences, their ignored dream.

In daylight the car hums. Bluevale    Seaforth
Newry    Holmesville.
The deer and flamingos, another mythology,
grace every tenth house.
This is not your home
but you are home.
                              Geraniums
in a tractor tire, horse weathervanes.
Moon over the Maitland River ...

And so that yellow light
man or woman working inside
aware of the cricket night
*cricket cricket ... cicada?* he writes, she says
to no one but the page
black hallways behind him
and ahead the windowscreen and then
the yard of yellow highway into maple
which his mind can walk out on
and dream a story
for his friends, the community

as someone once imagined
a dancing cow, a giant cheese.
The dream made name.
The gestures of the barroom
made dictionary.

*iii.*

When the four piece band sat stony in the Blyth Hotel
and played *Maple Sugar,* the bar got up to dance.
My shoulder banging against the women's room
to avoid flying drunk feet in their boots
that brought the cowshit in. And the bullshit
came too, through the beer and smoke.

This lady on the electric piano, the two fiddlers
and guitarist, the actors from across the street
stepping up to sing, receive stormy ovations.
The tv green and orange above us
recording grade B Hollywood, flamingo art.
And something is happening here.
Town and actors exchanging clothes.
The mechanic holds his harmonica
professionally against the mike
piercing out 'Have you ever been lonely
have you ever been blue,'
and, as the man from Lobo says,
*Fuck the Renaissance*
*– just get me a beer.*

*iv.*

So this midnight choir.

At 2 a.m. everyone is thrown out
and spreads onto the empty streets.
Unseen, as we step into cars,
are the bear and hawk,
who generate us.
And from the unseen sky
the crow watches
traffic light up Highway 4
then turn into unpaved
yellow concession roads.

The car bounces on a grass path
between tall corn and stops.

Light from the open car
reveals the yard.
And, as if painted onto the night,
is the yellow window
where someone, holding a mirror
in her left hand,
is drawing a picture of herself.

## Red Accordion – an immigrant song

How you and I talked!
Casually, and side by side,
not even cold at 4 a.m.
New Year's morning

in a double outhouse in Blyth.

Creak of trees and scrub snow.
Was it dream or true memory
this casualness, this ease of talk
after the long night of the previous year.

Nothing important said
just as now the poem
draws together such frail times.
Art steps forward as accident
like a warm breeze from Brazil.

         This whispering
as if not to awaken
what hibernates in firewood
as if not to disturb the blue night
the last memory of the year.

         So we sit
within loose walls of the poem
you and I, our friends indoors
drunk on the home-made wine.
All of us searching to discern ourselves,
the 'gift' we can give each other.
Tell this landscape.
Or the one we came from.

Polkas in a smoky midnight light.

I stepped into this new year
dancing with a small child.
Rachel, so graceful,
we bowed when the dance was over.
If I could paint this I would

                and if writing
showed colour and incident
removed from time
                we could be clear.

The bleak view past the door
is where we are, not what we
have made here, or become, or brought
like wolves bringing food to a lair
from another world. And this
is magic.
                Ray Bird's seven year old wine
– transformed! Finally made good.
I drank an early version years ago
and passed out.
                Time collapses.
The years, the intricate
knowledge now of each other
makes love.

A yard in its scrub snow, stacked wood
brindle in the moonlight, the red truck,
a bare tree at the foot of the driveway
waving to heaven.
                A full moon the
                colour of night kitchen.

Ten yards away a high bonfire
(remembered from summer) lifts
its redness above the farmhouse
and the lean figures of children circle
to throw in sticks and arms off a christmas tree
as the woman in long black hair
her left foot on a stump
plays the red accordion.

And the others dance.
                    Embracing or flinging
themselves away from each other.
They bow and they look up
to full moon and white cold sky
and they *move,* even in this stilled painting.
They talk a white breath at each other.
Some appear more than once
with different partners.
We are immune to wind.
Our boots pound down the frozen earth
our children leap from and into our arms.
All of us poised and inspired by music
friendship self-made heat and the knowledge
each has chosen to come here driven for hours
over iced highways, to be here bouncing and leaping

to a reel that carried itself generations ago
north of the border, through lost towns,
settled among the strange names,
and became eventually our own

all the way from Virginia.

There was another reason for Fats Waller to record, on May 8th 1935, "I'm gonna sit right down and write myself a letter." It is for this moment, driving from Goderich towards and past Blyth, avoiding Blyth by taking the gravel concessions, four adults and a child, who have just swum in a very cold Lake Huron. His piano drips from the cassette player and we all recognize the piece but are mute. We cannot sing before he does, before he eases himself into the lyrics as if into a chair, this large man who is to die in 1943 sitting in a train in Kansas City, finally still.

He was always moving, grand on the street or the midnight taxi rides with Andy Razaf during which it is rumoured he wrote most of his songs. I have always loved him but I love him most in the company of friends. Because his body was a crowd and we desire to imitate such community. His voice staggers or is gentle behind a whimsical piano, the melody ornamental and cool as vichyssoise in that hot studio in this hot car on a late June Ontario summer day. What else of importance happened on May 8th, 1935?

The only creature I've ever met who disliked him was a nervous foxhound I had for three years. As soon as I put on Mr. Waller the dog would dart from the room and hide under a bed. The dog recognised the anarchy, the unfolding of musical order, the growls and muttering, the fact that Fats Waller was talking to someone over your shoulder as well as to you. What my dog did not notice was the serenity he should have learned from. The notes as fresh as creek washed clothes.

The windows are open as we drive under dark maples that

sniff up a rumour of Lake Huron. The piano energizes the hay bound into wheels, a white field of turkeys, various tributaries of the Maitland River. Does he, drunk, and carrying his tin of tomatoes – "it feeds the body and cuts the hangover" – does he, in the midnight taxi with Razaf, imagine where the music disappears? Where it will recur? Music and lyrics they wrote then sold to false composers for ready cash and only later admitting they had written "Sunny side of the street" and "I can't give you anything but love" and so many of the best songs of their time. The hidden authors on their two hour taxi ride out of Harlem to Brooklyn and back again to Harlem, the night heat and smells yells overhead from the streets they passed through which they incorporated into what they were making every texture entering this large man, a classical organist in his youth, who strode into most experiences, hid from his ex-wife Edith Hatchett, visiting two kinds of women, 'ladies who had pianos and ladies who did not,' and died of bronchial pneumonia on the Acheson-Topeka and Santa Fe, a song he did not write.

He and the orchestra of his voice have now entered the car with us. This is his first visit to the country, though he saw it from a train window the day before he died. Saw the heartland where the music could disappear, the diaspora of notes, a rewinding, a backward movement of the formation of the world, the invention of his waltz.

## When you drive the Queensborough roads at midnight

do not look at a star
or full moon. Look out for frogs.
And not the venerable ones who recline
on gravel parallel to the highway
but the foolhardy, bored on a country night
dazzled by the adventure of passing beams.

We know their type of course, local heroes
who take off their bandanas and leap naked,
night green, seduced
by the whispers of michelin.

To them we are distinct death.
I am fond of these foolish things
more than the moon.
They welcome me after absence.
One of them is my youth
still jumping into rivers
take care and beware of him.

Knowing you love this landscape
there are few rules.
Do not gaze at moons.
Nuzzle the heat in granite.
Swim toward pictographs.
Touch only reflections.

## Proust in the Waters

*for Scott and Krystyne*


Swimming along the bar of moon
the yellow scattered sleeping
arm of the moon
                on Balsam Lake

releasing the air
                out of your mouth
the moon under your arm
tick of the brain
submerged. Tick
of the loon's heart
in the wet night thunder
                            below us
knowing its shore is the air

We love things which disappear
and are found
creatures who plummet
and become
an arrow.
To know the syllables
in a loon sentence
                intricate
shift of preposition
that signals meridian
                west    south west.
The mother tongue
a bubble caught in my beak
releasing the air
                of a language

Seeing no human in this moon storm
being naked in black water
you approach the corridor
such jewellery! Queen Anne's Lace!
and slide to fathoms, androgynous.
The mouth swallows river morse
throws a sound
through the loom of liquid
against sky.

*Where are you?*

*On the edge*
*of the moon bar*

## Birch Bark

*for George Whalley*


An hour after the storm on Birch Lake
the island bristles. Rock. Leaves still falling.
At this time, in the hour after lightning
we release the canoes.
Silence of water
purer than the silence of rock.
A paddle touches itself. We move
over blind mercury, feel the muscle
within the river, the blade
weave in dark water.

Now each casual word is precisely chosen
passed from bow to stern, as if
leaning back to pass a canteen.
There are echoes, repercussions of water.
We are in absolute landscape,
among names that fold in onto themselves.

To circle the island means witnessing
the blue grey dust of a heron
released out of the trees.
So the dialogue slides
nothing more than friendship
an old song we break into
not needing all the words.

We are past naming the country.
The reflections are never there
without us, without the exhaustion
of water and trees after storm.

## Escarpment

He lies in bed, awake, holding her left forearm. It is 4 a.m. He turns, his eyes rough against the night. Through the window he can hear the creek – which has no name. Yesterday at noon he walked along its shallow body overhung with cedar, beside rushes, moss, and watercress. A green and grey body whose intricate bones he is learning among which he stumbles and walks through in an old pair of Converse running shoes. She was further upriver investigating for herself and he exploring on his own now crawling under a tree that has uprooted and spilled. Its huge length across a section of the creek. With his left hand he holds onto the massive stump roots and slides beneath it within the white water heaving against him. Shirt wet, he follows the muscle in the water and travels fast under the tree. His dreaming earlier must have involved all this.

In the river he was looking for a wooden bridge which they had crossed the previous day. He walks confidently now, the white shoes stepping casually off logs into deep water, through gravel, and watercress which they eat later in a cheese sandwich. She chews much of it walking back to the cabin. He turns and she freezes, laughing, with watercress in her mouth. There are not many more ways he can tell her he loves her. He shows mock outrage and yells but she cannot hear him over the sound of the stumbling creek.

He loves too, as she knows, the body of rivers. Provide him with a river or a creek and he will walk along it. Will step off and sink to his waist, the sound of water and rock encasing him in solitude. The noise around them insists on silence if they are more than five feet apart. It is only later when they sit in a pool legs against each other that they can talk, their conversation roaming to include relatives, books, best friends, the history of Lewis and Clark, fragments of the past which they piece together. But otherwise this river's noise encases them and now he walks alone with its spirits, the clack and splash, the twig break, hearing only an individual noise if it occurs less than an arm's length away. He is looking, now, for a name.

It is not a name for a map – he knows the arguments of imperialism. It is a name for them, something temporary for their vocabulary. A code. He slips under the fallen tree holding the cedar root the way he holds her forearm. He hangs a moment, his body being pulled by water going down river. He holds it the same way and for the same reasons. Heart Creek? Arm River? he writes, he mutters to her in the darkness. The body moves from side to side and he hangs with one arm, deliriously out of control, still holding on. Then he plunges down, touches gravel and flakes of wood with his back the water closing over his head like a clap of gloved hands. His eyes are open as the river itself pushes him to his feet and he is already three yards down stream and walking out of the shock and cold stepping into the sun. Sun lays its crossword, litters itself, along the whole turning length of this river so he can step into heat or shadow.

He thinks of where she is, what she is naming. Near her, in the grasses, are Bladder Campion, Devil's Paintbrush, some unknown blue flowers. He stands very still and cold in the shadow of long trees. He has gone far enough to look for a bridge and has not found it. Turns upriver. He holds onto the cedar root the way he holds her forearm.

Thanks to the editors of the following magazines and chapbooks who first published some of these poems: *Brick, Now, Canadian Forum, Malahat Review, Descant, Island, Epoch, Ethos, This Magazine, Canadian Literature,* Coach House Press Manuscript Editions, and Island Press.

Two poems, 'The River Neighbour' and 'Pacific Letter', are based on Rihaku – Tu Fu – Pound poems. They are not so much translations as re-locations into my landscape, the earlier poets making their appearance in these poems.

A line by Rilke and a line by James Wright make up titles in the *Rock Bottom* section. The last line in the 'George' poem is by John Berryman.

The Man from Lobo is Don McKay. With thanks.

'The Cinnamon Peeler' and 'Women like You' appeared first in *Running in the Family* published by McClelland and Stewart.

Thanks to the Ontario Arts Council and the Canada Council who have supported me at various stages.

Thanks to my friends in the clutch.

Bellrock-Toronto-Honolulu-Colombo-
Blyth-Collingwood-Madoc
1978-1983

\*

Editor for the Press: Sarah Sheard
Typeset in Galliard and printed in Canada

Also available from Coach House Talking Books

*Previous Canoes* by Michael Ondaatje
Poetry selected and read by the author includes sections of
*Secular Love.*

Poetry 90 minutes (1 cassette) $14.95 0-88910-394-1

COACH HOUSE PRESS
401 (rear) Huron Street
Toronto, Canada M5S 2G5